# Lost in a Blizzard!

## THE TOWNER BUS TRAGEDY

ALYCE MITCHEM JENKINS

**Perfection Learning**®

Cover design and inside layout: Michelle J. Glass

## Dedication

I dedicate this book to the memory of my parents, John "Foster" Mitchem and Queenie Black Mitchem, whose experiences in eastern Colorado became part of my life and provided my inspiration.

## About the Author

Alyce Mitchem Jenkins grew up in "The Milk Center of the World." A statue of a black-and-white cow greets visitors to her hometown, Harvard, Illinois.

Alyce has taught English and social studies in Colorado, Illinois, Wisconsin, Ohio, and New Jersey, where she presently lives. She enjoys writing for children's magazines because she gets to interview neat kids as well as TV stars and professional athletes. She also leads an adoption support group and is an avid women's basketball fan.

Now that son David and daughter Beth are grown, Alyce and her husband adore "spoiling" granddaughters Skyler and Sierra.

# ACKNOWLEDGMENTS

Many people have helped me prepare this book. Special thanks to Nadine Cheney, curator of the Horace Greeley Museum in Tribune, Kansas, who devoted days to guiding me through the Pleasant Hill School region and sharing her extensive collection of clippings and articles about the Towner Bus Tragedy as well as her expertise about life in eastern Colorado and western Kansas. Thanks also to Ormal Humburg, whose interviews and narration during our tour of the bus route provided a great deal of information and understanding about life on the prairie in 1931. And to Ruthanna Jacobs of the Kiowa County Historical Society in Eads, Colorado, who shared resources and typed articles for me. Betty Talbert and Dixie Scott of Cheyenne County provided articles and other resources to help me begin my research.

I am deeply indebted to the living survivors of the lost bus, who generously granted me interviews and read and critiqued my manuscript despite the tears and painful memories that the story evoked. Rosemary Brown Cannon, Maxine Brown Foreman, Alice Huffaker Huggins, Charles Huffaker, Laura Huffaker Loehr, Blanche Stonebraker Widger, and Eunice Frost Youkey are gracious, kind, and good-humored individuals whom I greatly admire.

I thank Georgene Pearson, author of *A Light in the Window*, who offered her encouragement and shared resources with me. Other individuals whose writings guided me to make the story as factual as possible include Alice Spencer Cook, E. N. Coons, John Kenneth Herrick, Howard Huddleston, Joyce E. Huddleston, W. L. Liggett, Pansy Mosher, Nell Brown Propst, Edna Coons Reinert, Roleta D. Teal and contributors to *History of Early Greeley County: A Story of Its Tracks, Trials, and Tribulations* published by Greeley County Historical Book Committee (Vol. 1, 1981), and *Kiowa County* compiled by Roleta D. Teal, and Betty Jacobs and published by the Kiowa County Bicentennial Committee (1976), and *Kiowa County Colorado Centennial History* published by the Kiowa County Historical Society— Ruthanna Jacobs, Project Director (1989). In addition, "The School Bus to Hell" by Clark Secrest, published in *Colorado Heritage* (Winter 1994) provided some updated details.

I am indebted to the Warren Writers, my loyal friends and critics, whose suggestions I respected and incorporated into my manuscript. I am grateful for the patience and care of my editors at Perfection Learning Corporation, Sue Thies and Judy Bates, and Randy Messer and Michelle Glass of the art department, who brought the story to life in a visual manner. And most of all, I thank my husband, Dr. Reese V. Jenkins, and my adult children, David and Beth, who have encouraged my writing through the years.

*Alyce Mitchem Jenkins*
April 2000

# TABLE OF CONTENTS

# AUTHOR'S NOTE

I grew up in northern Illinois, not on the prairies of western Kansas and eastern Colorado. But for five years before I was born, my mother and father lived in Cheyenne Wells, Colorado.

Mother was from Chicago. How different and wonderful she found life in a tiny town in eastern Colorado! She told me so many stories that her experiences there became part of my life too.

Mother often warned me about the dangers of winter. "No matter how cold you are, never lie down and go to sleep!" she'd say. Then she told me about the busload of kids lost in a blizzard.

I wanted to know more. Who were they? Why were they lost? For how long? Who rescued them? Why did one boy get national attention as a hero? What happened to the others? I wrote this book to answer my questions.

Some details have been fictionalized to convey the lifestyle of the early 1930s. They have been added, along with some dialogue, as if they definitely occurred on March 26, 1931. People and events are factual.

# INTRODUCTION

Imagine you're on a school bus with 19 other kids. School is out early. Everyone is singing and laughing. You can't wait to get home and play.

But snow is falling. The wind is blowing fiercely. Blowing snow rushes sideways through the air. Snow is even blowing into your bus through broken windows.

Your bus driver can't see anything out the front window. You're lost!

Suddenly you feel a bump. The bus has slipped into a ditch. It's stuck. The motor dies. The wind is roaring outside. The bus is getting colder and colder. You must get help.

But you have no telephone. Your parents think you're safe at school. They won't come looking for you. In fact, no one will go out in such a storm. You may freeze to death!

On March 26, 1931, that's exactly what happened. A bus driver and 20 Colorado children were trapped in their school bus during a **blizzard**.

## chapter

# Rosemary: Off to School

**Thursday, March 26, 1931**

"Time to get up, Maxine!" Thirteen-year-old Rosemary Brown poked her little sister. Maxine was lying beside Rosemary in bed.

There was no door between the kitchen and bedroom in the Browns' two-room dugout. Rosemary could see Mom fixing breakfast. It must already be 6 a.m. They'd have to hurry to catch the school bus.

## Dugout Homes

There weren't many trees in western Kansas and eastern Colorado. Settlers dug about four feet below ground to make small one- or two-room homes.

Dugouts didn't cost much to build. People cemented the floor and lined the walls with **adobe** bricks. It was cheaper to **whitewash** the walls than to paint them. A stairway led up to a small entrance building. Some had a dug-out path leading to the doorway.

Above ground were small, narrow windows. A pitched roof started about two feet above ground. It was covered with tar paper and **sod**.

Below ground, the families were protected from the harsh cold and blowing snow of **prairie** winters. In summer, the cool earth kept away the sun's hot rays.

March 26, 1931, started out like any other day. As soon as eight-year-old Maxine hopped out of bed, Rosemary pulled up Mom's handmade quilts.

"Here, Maxine! Help me close the bed," she said.

Soon their bed was a sofa again. But the little room was still crowded. Mom and Daddy's bed was near the sofa.

Rosemary's older brothers, Harold and Roy, and 11-year-old Bobbie would be coming in soon for breakfast. They'd be anxious to get warm. The boys slept in a small, unheated building near the dugout.

Rosemary had worn long underwear all winter. But not today! The last few days had been warm. It was finally spring!

Instead, Rosemary pulled up her long brown cotton stockings. "Dirty brown!" she called them. She fastened them on to her **garter belt**.

Then Rosemary stepped into a cotton skirt. She pulled a sweater over her head.

"This sweater is too big!" she said to herself. Its sleeves almost covered her hands. But it would have to do. She put on brown **oxford** shoes and quickly brushed her short brown hair.

Rosemary didn't have many clothes. Anyway, she had nowhere to keep clothes. The small dugout didn't have closets.

A warm breeze was blowing from the south as Rosemary hurried to the **outhouse**. No time today to read the Sears, Roebuck catalog!

Sears, Roebuck and Montgomery Ward sent free catalogs to homes. During hard times, many people didn't have money to buy unnecessary items. So they used the pages from the catalogs as bathroom tissue.

8

On the way back, Rosemary noticed that the sky was almost yellow. The air was hazy. She joined Mom and Maxine in the small kitchen.

"It looks strange outside, Mom," Rosemary said. "Maybe the dust is blowing."

"Oh, no!" her mother replied. "I sure hope not!"

Within a couple of years, the region where the Browns lived would become part of an area called the "Dust Bowl." Because there was little rain, the topsoil blew through the air. People couldn't even see through the clouds of dirt.

Mom had soaked whole wheat grain in water all night. Now she was boiling it to make cereal. Maxine was setting the large wooden table.

"Rosemary, please bring in milk, butter, eggs, and bacon," Mom said.

Rosemary went to the cool entryway to get the food. Extra eggs, milk, and cream were kept in the well house. When the wind blew, the windmill pumped cool water. It flowed into a trough. There the food was kept fresh, even in the summer.

Just then Bobbie brought in a pail of water. Sometimes Rosemary carried water the 100 feet from the well to the house. She took the pail from her brother. Then she heated the water on the coal stove.

## Children's Chores on the Prairie

Young people living on the prairie had little time to play. They did chores before and after school.

The boys helped care for livestock and worked in the fields. Girls gathered eggs and helped their mothers cook, sew, and clean.

After school, the girls had other chores. For example, Rosemary had to clean the cream **separators**. First, the disks were removed and rinsed in cold water. Then they were washed with soap and hot water and rinsed again. Rosemary dried them with feed-sack towels that she had **embroidered**.

After supper, the children did homework. Without electricity, they read by the light of **coal oil** lamps. The lamp chimneys had to be cleaned and the lamps filled with fuel often. The children went to bed early, usually by 8 p.m.

Mom was frying bacon and eggs in a large iron pan. She took hot biscuits from the oven.

Soon Daddy and the other boys came in.

"It's pretty warm out," Daddy said. "But there are unusual-looking low clouds on the **horizon**. I sure hope the sun breaks through soon."

Rosemary hoped so too. Then she and her friends could play outside during recess.

The Browns joined hands around the wooden table. Daddy thanked God for their food and for another day. Breakfast was their big meal together.

"Come on, boys. Let's get the chores done," Daddy said after breakfast was finished. Harold, Roy, and Bobbie hurried outside. Rosemary noticed Bobbie had on a light jacket.

Quickly, Maxine cleared the table. Rosemary washed the dishes with homemade soap in the pan of water she'd heated.

Then she rinsed them in another pan of hot water. Quickly, she dried the dishes and put them away.

Mom and Maxine packed the kids' lunches. First, Mom made peanut butter and egg sandwiches on homemade bread. Then Maxine put them in a large gallon syrup bucket. Next she slipped in pieces of rich chocolate cake. After Christmas, there might have been oranges or bananas from the kids' stockings. But not today. The Browns couldn't afford store-bought fruit very often.

"Come on! The bus will be here soon!" Rosemary and Maxine put on their coats and hurried out the door. Bobbie had finished **slopping** the pigs. He joined them. Roy and Harold stayed home to help with the farmwork.

"Bobbie, it might storm. Better wear your warmer jacket!" Mom called.

"It's warm out, Mom," Bobbie called back. "I'll be OK."

The small bus turned around in the Browns' driveway. It was really a 1929 six-cylinder Chevrolet truck.

On the truck bed stood a wooden frame with windows in front and back and along both sides. To the driver's right was a wooden door with a window. A five-gallon cream can was strapped onto the **running board**. It carried water for school. Inside the bus, two long benches faced each other.

Rosemary never complained about the strange bus. Last year, when her family had lived farther east, the children had walked a mile to school every day. Now, as an eighth grader, she liked riding to school with her best friends.

# Transportation to School

**Rural** school buses were not common on the plains in 1931. To get to school, most children either walked across the open fields, rode horseback, or rode in horse-drawn wagons or buggies.

Parents often kept children home until they were seven or eight years old. Then they were big enough for the long walk to school.

Near many rural schools was a shed. There the pupils' horses were fed and rested while the children attended school.

"Good morning, children!" Carl Miller said as he opened the bus door. He picked up the Brown children first each day. Greeley County, Kansas, where they lived, paid for them to go to Pleasant Hill School in Colorado, only five miles away.

"Good morning, Mr. Miller," Rosemary said. She liked her bus driver. He was a rancher just like Daddy. Besides, he was the father of Mary Louise, one of her schoolmates.

Sometimes Mary Louise didn't come with her dad. Instead, she watched her little brother, Louis, while Mrs. Miller did chores. Then she'd get on the bus when it passed the Miller house.

Rosemary sat on one bench. Maxine and Bobbie sat across from her on the other side. The two were close in age, so they were playmates.

Rosemary glanced to the back of the bus. Someone had covered the broken back windows with cardboard.

That won't keep bad weather out! Rosemary thought.

Front row, left to right: Charles, Alice, Gladys, Max, and Carl Huffaker. Back row, left to right: Mrs. Huffaker, Lena, and Mr. Huffaker. Photo was taken before Laura and Robert were born. The Huffakers are in front of their partially completed dugout house, in late summer of 1922.

chapter 2

# Charles: All Aboard the Bus!

About a mile down the road, 13-year-old Charles Huffaker and his brothers Carl, age 11, and Max, age 10, got up about six o'clock.

The children's parents had come to Kansas in a covered wagon in 1914 to **homestead**. Mr. Huffaker built a dugout. Later, as their family grew, he added an above-ground kitchen and bedroom. The boys shared a bed downstairs in the underground part.

Like Bobbie Brown, the Huffaker boys milked the cows and slopped the pigs before school. The night before they'd brought in water from the well that was about 25 feet from the house. They'd poured the water into the **reservoir** on the stove. As the fire burned in the stove, the water heated.

# Fuel

Coal was a common fuel for these families. They bought it or picked it up along the railroad tracks. Corncobs, left after the pigs ate the corn, were less expensive and easy to burn.

Families also burned **cow chips** in their stoves. These chips were often called *prairie coal*. Children collected the chips in baskets or **gunnysacks** after they had dried. Their parents hauled the cow chips home in a horse-drawn wagon and stacked them. Each evening, a family member brought coal, corncobs, or cow chips in for the stoves.

The Huffaker boys were joined by sisters Gladys, age 17; Alice, age 14; Lena, age 9; and Laura, age 7; and 4-year-old Robert. They ate a hearty breakfast of milk, eggs, gravy, butter, biscuits, and bacon. Their baby sister was still asleep.

# Prairie Life

Many families produced most of what they needed. Their cows gave milk and beef. Pigs provided bacon, pork, and **lard**. The families had chickens and eggs too. Large gardens grew nearby.

Fruit trees didn't grow well on the prairie. So apples and peaches were shipped in during the late summer. Mrs. Huffaker and many other women canned vegetables, fruit, and meat.

The women made soap from lard and **lye**. Women also made bread for their families. Mrs. Huffaker baked eight loaves of bread and either doughnuts or cinnamon buns two or three times each week. Kitchen stoves had no heat controls. But the women knew how much fuel was needed to bake at the right temperatures.

Once a week, the men drove wagons or cars to the nearest town. Often it took them an hour or more each way.

In town, the men **bartered** items, such as cream or eggs, for flour, sugar, salt, coffee, cornmeal, peanut butter, crackers, shoes, lye, or other things the family needed. After harvest, there might be extra wheat or corn to sell or trade too.

The women made their boys' shirts and girls' dresses. Chicken feed came in patterned cloth bags. The women bought enough bags of the same design to make a dress or shirt. Flour and sugar sacks provided fabric for light underwear and towels.

Women and the older girls sewed by hand or on **treadle** sewing machines. Families also ordered goods from Sears, Roebuck or Montgomery Ward catalogs.

After breakfast, Charles put a cotton shirt over his **long handles**. He stepped into his overalls. The Huffaker children's clothes were not new. But they were always clean.

# Clothing Care

Washing clothes was a big job in 1931. A rancher's wife usually washed on a day with enough wind to run the windmill that pumped the water. Otherwise, she had to pump the water by hand.

Some women had "modern" washing machines. They cranked the machines by hand to swish the water and clothes.

Other women had to heat water in a big boiler and wash clothes with **washboards**. Sometimes they boiled the white clothes to get them clean.

Then the dresses and shirts were **starched**. The clothes dried outside on clotheslines. Later, they were dampened and ironed with flat

irons. The irons were placed on top of the cooking stoves to heat. In the Browns' home, the stove was kerosene-heated. There was no way to control the heat so it was easy to **scorch** the clothes.

Girls always wore dresses to school. Boys' overalls were either purchased or sewn at home.

Clothes had to last a long time. The women mended holes in the knees. The children wore lots of **hand-me-downs**.

"It doesn't matter how it looks as long as it's clean," some mothers told their children.

Meanwhile, Charles's sisters and their mom packed meat sandwiches and cookies.

"I'm taking popcorn today!" Laura announced. Instead of a lunch bucket, she had a paper bag.

"Better wear your jackets," Mom said. "It just might storm!"

All six of the Huffaker children going to school put on warm jackets. Max wore high rubber boots with no shoes. Charles wore just high-top shoes.

Outdoors, Charles noticed dark clouds overhead. They were blowing through the sky. Dirt was blowing too.

But Charles didn't worry. The bus was coming from the Browns' house.

Last year, Charles had walked two miles across fields to New Hope School. This year he went to school in the same building. But it had been moved to Pleasant Hill School. Riding the bus was great.

Charles behaved and worked hard at school. His mom and dad saw to it that he always did his homework. And if he got a spanking at school, he got a worse one at home.

But Charles was waiting for summer. He looked forward to vacation!

"Good morning!" Mr. Miller greeted the Huffaker children. "It's going to be a great spring day!"

Rosemary patted the bench. She wanted Alice to join her. Alice's blonde hair bounced. Her blue eyes sparkled as she greeted her friend.

# The Rest of the Kids

About a mile farther down the road, Mr. Miller stopped for the Frosts. They were Charles's first cousins. Eunice, age 14, and Leland, age 7, were both wearing four-buckle overshoes.

Their older sisters were married. So the younger Frost children were close. Eunice had played school with Leland and taught him how to read.

The Frost family had lived in a dugout until their dad built an above-ground house for the chickens. But it was so much nicer than the family's house that chickens never lived there. Instead, the family did.

Remains of an above-ground house, typical of this period in time

Later, Mr. Frost added more rooms. The cool dugout became a place to store milk, cream, butter, and eggs.

Next to board the bus was 13-year-old Louise Stonebraker and her 10-year-old sister, Blanche. The Stonebrakers lived in a two-story wooden house.

Site of the Stonebrakers' house

On holidays, Rosemary, Louise, Eunice, and Alice loved to walk or ride their horses together in a pasture between their houses. Patsy, the Browns' strawberry **roan**, enjoyed the outings as much as Rosemary did.

Sometimes, the friends played hide-and-seek. Or they popped corn, chatted, and giggled about what was happening at home and school.

Today, Louise had no jacket. She only wore a bulky-knit sweater.

It's so warm. I really don't need my coat either, Rosemary thought. Louise joined her and the others on the bench.

Farther along, seven-year-old Kenneth Johnson was waiting outside his stone house. Kenneth had been adopted. He had no brothers or sisters. He was one of the youngest children on the bus.

Next, eight-year-old Mary Louise Miller came running to the bus. Her coat was unbuttoned. "Hi, Daddy," Mary Louise said as she hopped on. From the window, she waved good-bye to her little brother, Louis, who stood by their mother.

Next, the bus stopped at the four-room **bungalow** of the Untiedt family. Bryan was almost thirteen. Ten-year-old Evelyn, nine-year-old Ome, and eight-year-old Arlo jumped on board with Bryan.

"Where's Virgil?" someone asked. Bryan's 11-year-old brother wasn't with them.

"He's sick. Lucky kid!" Bryan replied, laughing. Little did anyone know how lucky Virgil really was.

Clara Smith also got on. Clara, already 15, was working for the Untiedts. She helped Mrs. Untiedt cook, wash, clean, and care for her new baby.

Clara's sister, Nora, lived with another family west of the school. So she didn't ride Mr. Miller's bus at all.

Now 20 children were crowded onto the two benches in the small bus. They talked and laughed about what they'd be doing at school. And they talked about the heroes in their lives.

Class Photo

*Front row, left to right:*
Leland Frost, Kearney Burton, Arlo Untiedt, Kenneth Johnson, Laura Huffaker, Mary Louise Miller, Lena Huffaker

*Middle row, left to right:*
Ralph Smith, Roy Bond, Maxine Brown

*Back row, left to right:*
Blanche Stonebraker, Max Huffaker, Robert Brown, Carl Huffaker, Louis Smith, Evelyn Untiedt, Wanda Crum, Ome Untiedt

*Those on the school bus but not pictured:*
Carl Miller, Louise Stonebraker, Rosemary Brown, Eunice Frost, Alice Huffaker, Charles Huffaker, Clara Smith, Bryan Untiedt

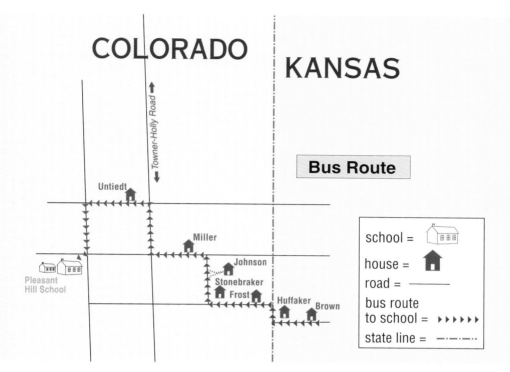

**COLORADO**    **KANSAS**

Towner-Holly Road

**Bus Route**

Untiedt

Miller

Johnson

Pleasant
Hill School

Stonebraker

Frost

Huffaker    Brown

school = 
house = 
road = ———
bus route
to school = ▸▸▸▸▸▸
state line = —··—··—··

## Heroes

A *hero* is someone whom people admire for doing something special or showing courage. Children today find their heroes in movies and on TV. Sports figures are heroes too. Books, videos, computer games, and comics also provide hero figures.

*Charles Lindbergh*

Without radios, newspapers, or TV, rural children of 1931 found their heroes in their school lessons. They respected leaders like George Washington, Abraham Lincoln, and Thomas Edison. They also liked Calvin Coolidge and Herbert Hoover, the United States presidents of their time.

Other heroes included Henry Ford, who had made it possible for their families to have cars. Charles Lindbergh was admired as the first person to fly alone across the Atlantic Ocean. Amelia Earhart, the first woman to pilot a plane across the Atlantic, became a hero. Will Rogers was respected because he made people laugh.

*Amelia Earhart*

Also, parents and teachers were heroes to the children. "My mother was a magician," Rosemary once said. "She could do a lot with very little."

Children living in towns and cities saw movies and listened to radio more than rural children did. Their heroes probably included the Lone Ranger, Colleen Moore, Helen Morgan, Tom Mix, and Gary Cooper. Important sports heroes included baseball player Babe Ruth and boxer Gene Tunney.

Babe Ruth

On March 26, 1931, twenty students were having fun on their way to school. They hardly noticed the dark clouds on the northwest horizon and the falling snow.

# chapter 4

# Hurray! No School Today!

Carl Miller pulled up to the two buildings that made up Pleasant Hill School. The building on the left, once New Hope School, was the junior high. Mr. Freiday taught the older kids there.

To the right was the larger building. Grades one through six studied together in one room. Their teacher, Mrs. Moser, was new that year. Behind the buildings were two outhouses. One was for

the boys. The other was for the girls. In between was the coal shed.

Pleasant Hill was a strange name. There was no hill—only flat prairie in all directions. There were no flowers, trees, or even a well. But it was a pleasant place for Rosemary. She loved school, especially math and English.

On weekends Rosemary's family attended Sunday school and church in the school buildings. Sometimes a traveling minister preached. Other Sundays, Rosemary's father led the services. Rosemary loved the singing.

Often church families got together for covered-dish dinners. These gave the young people a chance to talk and play.

Mrs. Moser

# Rural Fun

The students at Pleasant Hill School knew one another well. Children living in the country seldom went to town except at special times, such as the 4th of July. Then families drove to Holly, Colorado, to watch the parade and gunnysack races.

With no TV or nearby movies, the people of the Pleasant Hill area made their own fun. They held dances in someone's barn that had a loft for the musicians. Rosemary's dad played the fiddle. The young people also danced outdoors while they sang songs like "Skip to My Lou."

At pie or box suppers, each girl packed a lunch or made a pie and decorated the box to hold it. Then the boys bid on the box they wanted. The highest bidder ate what was inside with the girl who had fixed it. A girl felt really proud if her box brought a whole dollar!

The children didn't have many toys. During school vacations, the children looked for birds' eggs and snakes. They often rode horseback. And sometimes, just for fun, they poured water in **prairie dog** holes!

The children did enjoy holiday programs at school and church.

Rosemary, Charles, and the other children hurried off the bus. Snow was collecting on the ground.

"Let's play fox and geese!" someone shouted. The older kids stamped a large circle in the snow. Across the middle, they made paths like wheel spokes.

Charles was the "fox." He tried to catch a "goose." If he did, that person became the next fox.

The youngsters laughed and shouted as they chased around the circle and raced to the center to be "safe." It didn't matter if they fell and got wet. Soon they could warm up inside the school.

# Children's Games

There were no swings or slides at Pleasant Hill School. Children of all ages played together in the dirt school yard. In 1931, American children enjoyed jumping rope and throwing horseshoes. They also played checkers, marbles, jacks, mumblety-peg, tiddledywinks, blindman's bluff, ring-around-the-rosy, farmer in the dell, fox and geese, Annie-Annie-over, and drop the handkerchief. Often the children scratched hopscotch boxes into the playground dirt.

Sometimes all the children had was a ball of string and a large stick. So they'd play baseball!

For a while, no one noticed that children from west of the school had not come. Nor did they notice that the wind had shifted to the north. The snow was getting heavier. And it was getting colder.

At the same time, Mr. Miller carried the can of water into the school. He had to pour it into two buckets, one for each building. If the kids got thirsty, they dipped a tin cup into the bucket to get a drink. And they all used the same tin cup! Water poured into a **basin** became their sink.

Usually Mr. Miller returned to the bus. He had farmwork to do. But today, he stayed in the school.

Outside, Rosemary was shivering. A cold wind cut through her coat. She pulled her long sweater over her hands. But the cold ripped right through her cotton dress and stockings.

Charles's jacket wasn't warm enough either. "Let's go inside!" he shouted. The others followed him into the grade school building.

But classes weren't ready to start. Instead, Mr. Freiday, Mrs. Moser, and Mr. Miller were talking. Sometimes one of them walked over and looked out the window at the heavy dark clouds in the northwest.

Then the adult voices rose. Mr. Miller seemed to be disagreeing with what the teachers were saying. Finally, he picked up the cream can and headed back to the bus.

Mr. Freiday rapped a ruler on Mrs. Moser's desk. "A bad storm may be coming," he said. "This building gets cold in a storm, even with our coal stove. And snow comes in around the windows. Besides, we don't have enough food to stay here long."

Mr. Freiday continued. "Boys, please bring in coal for tomorrow. Everyone else, take your books and papers and get back on the bus. Mr. Miller will take you home."

## Weather Forecasts

### In 1931

Weather was important to farmers and ranchers. Their crops depended on rain, sun, and heat.

Some families on the Colorado prairie had battery-operated radios. But the sound didn't come in clearly. With difficulty, they listened to favorite programs like *Amos 'n' Andy* and *The National Barn Dance*. They couldn't afford to run the radios very much. So they often didn't hear weather forecasts.

The families didn't get daily newspapers, either. In the Pleasant Hill community, only the family of Louise and Blanche Stonebraker had a telephone. Neither buses nor rural schools had telephones or radios.

Without contact with the outside world, ranchers and their families had to use other things to know what the weather would be. They watched the sky, checked thermometers and **barometers**, and looked at **weather vanes**. They also read the **almanac**.

Many people believed in weather lore. Some people said that cattle were more lively before a storm. Others thought that two or three days after a coyote howled, the weather would change. Birds often flew south before a cold spell.

So the people guessed what weather was coming. These guesses weren't very exact. And sometimes they came too late!

## Today

In 1931, the United States Weather Service forecast weather based mostly on reports from weather balloons and people living in various places. Today, **meteorologists** study pictures from weather **satellites** and radar. They learn the location, direction, and speed of blizzards. Computers help meteorologists predict what will happen.

Meteorologists issue a blizzard watch if conditions are right for a storm. A blizzard warning says that a blizzard is probably coming or is already happening.

We still can't stop blizzards and other bad storms. But we can make wise decisions and prepare to deal with unsafe weather conditions.

"Hurray! No school today!" the kids shouted. They clapped their hands and hopped and skipped around.

Quickly, Charles and the older boys buttoned their jackets. The wind almost blew them to the coal house. They filled their **scuttles**. Then they struggled, slipped, and slid their way back to the school. How the wind and blowing snow made their eyes sting and water!

At the same time, the girls set out for the bus. The wind whipped the snow in their faces. The younger children could hardly walk.

Rosemary sat near the front of the bus. As Alice neared the bus, she could barely see her hand in front of her face because of the blowing snow.

Soon the boys joined the girls. Safe inside, everyone laughed and joked. They were going home!

It was about 9 a.m. Carl Miller set the spark and throttle levers in the bus. Then he went outside and turned the crank. The motor started.

Quickly, the bus driver wiped the piling snow off the windshield with his gloved hand. He got back inside and set out to take the kids home.

Mr. Miller thought the kids should have stayed at school. But the teachers wanted him to take them home. To hurry, he decided to take a shortcut to the Untiedts' house. Instead of following the road, he turned northeast along an unfenced trail. On the **open range**, the bus could drive right across the fields.

The storm was coming from the north. So the bus was heading right into the blowing snow!

Right away, Charles knew they were lost. Dirt, snow, and **tumbleweeds** were blowing through the air. Rosemary couldn't even see the top on the radiator tank just outside the window.

Mr. Miller couldn't see the trail either. "Help me keep on the road, kids!" he called.

The youngsters wiped off the clouded windows with their bare hands. Mr. Miller rolled down a front window. A gale of freezing air hit Rosemary in the face. Dirt and snow were blowing into the bus. Still, Mr. Miller could see nothing but snow.

"I'm cold," Maxine complained. "I want to go home!"

"Me too," Laura added.

"I'll take you back to school," Mr. Miller suggested. "We'll be warm there!"

Mr. Miller turned the bus around. He drove very slowly. But he didn't know which way the school was. His tire tracks had been covered by the blowing snow.

Finally, the bus bumped in and out of a ditch and up onto a road.

We're on the Towner-Holly Road, Mr. Miller thought. He'd take the kids to his house. Mrs. Miller and Louis would be glad to see them. Then they'd be warm and safe until the storm ended.

Mr. Miller turned right. A short time later, he turned left. But the bus wasn't where he thought it was.

The bus had passed close to the school before that left turn. Mr. Miller missed the one place where the children would be safe—the building they never should have left.

Mr. Miller was worried. The bus motor was sputtering. The wires were getting wet. But the kids were still having fun. Some of the boys were wrestling with one another. Everyone was shouting. The older girls began singing. Rosemary and her friends knew many songs.

Gone are the days, when my heart was young and gay. Gone are my friends, from the cotton fields away...

At first, Rosemary and Evelyn sang something different. They tried to drown out the others. Then everyone sang together.

Suddenly, the bus jerked. Everyone was tossed about. Some of the little kids fell off the benches.

"What happened?" Charles asked.

"Where are we, Mr. Miller?" Rosemary asked.

The singing had stopped. The children were quiet. Even the bus was silent. Its motor had died. The bus was stuck in a snowy **borrow pit**.

Carl Miller checked his watch. It was 11 a.m. They had been on the bus for two hours.

"I'm not sure where we are. But I'll get the bus started again," Mr. Miller said.

He got out and turned the crank. He tried to start the engine again and again. But it wouldn't start.

Mr. Miller looked around. He couldn't see anything he knew. In fact, he couldn't see anything at all. Blinding, blowing snow stung his face and eyes. It was as if he were playing blindman's bluff. And he couldn't get the blindfold off.

Mr. Miller had lived in the Pleasant Hill area for less than a year. Some of the kids had lived there much longer. Maybe they'd know where the bus was.

"Clara! Bryan!" Mr. Miller called. "Go out a little ways and look for something you recognize."

Quickly, Bryan and Clara stepped off the bus. But the powdery snow blew into their faces. They could hardly breathe. A white curtain blocked their view just like the curtains that divided rooms in their homes. They could see nothing. They climbed back onto the little bus.

Bryan was wearing only a light suit jacket. "Boy, it's cold!" he said, shivering.

Mr. Miller took off his warm jacket and gave it to Bryan. The boy quickly put it on.

The children remained quiet. They were cold, and they were scared. Maybe they wouldn't get home at all.

# chapter 5

# WHITEOUT!

Carl Miller knew they were in trouble. The snow wasn't deep. But the air had become so cold that the snow was dry and powdery.

Outside, he couldn't see. And he couldn't breathe either. Blowing snow could **suffocate** the kids and him if they left the bus.

Snow was blowing into the bus. The pieces of cardboard over the back windows didn't keep it out. And each time someone opened the bus door, more snow and cold air blew in.

Mr. Miller knew something the children didn't. The wind was so strong and the temperature so low that they could all freeze to death. Quickly, he pushed back the two benches to make room in the little bus. The children's lunches fell off behind the benches. But no one noticed.

"We've got to keep moving!" Mr. Miller said.

The 20 children bounced on their seats and pretended to fight. They marched around and around in the small space between the benches. This was fun! But it didn't last long.

"I'm still cold!" Maxine wailed.

"I'll start a fire," Mr. Miller said. He went outside into the storm again. He broke up the boards that held the can of water.

Mr. Miller climbed back onto the bus. He put the boards into an empty milk can lid. Then he struck a match and lighted a fire.

All 20 children tried to stand around the small fire. It was really crowded. So they had to take turns.

The children would march for a while. Then they'd snuggle up to the fire. But it didn't give off much heat. Besides, the wood was wet. The fire was smoking. Some of the kids began to cough.

Soon the boards were burned up. "Give me your books and papers!" Mr. Miller said. He threw the children's school supplies into the fire.

"No homework tonight!" Charles yelled.

But the books and papers were wet too. Smoke filled the bus. Now everyone was coughing.

Mr. Miller opened the door. The kids opened windows. More cold air and snow blew in. Then there were no more matches—and nothing left to burn.

# chapter 6

# Broken-Down And Lost

A swirling white enemy trapped the children on the cold little bus. But snow kept invading it. There was no escape.

Charles wondered when his mom and dad would miss him and his brothers and sisters. Maybe his aunt and uncle would come looking for Eunice and Leland.

Kenneth comforted his best friend. He put his arm around Arlo's shoulders and said that his daddy would find them.

The smaller children started to whine.

"I'm hungry," someone said.

"I want my popcorn!" Laura agreed.

Rosemary thought about her sandwiches. A piece of chocolate cake would taste great right now.

The kids raced to find their lunches. But the lunch buckets were stuck under frozen snow. There was nothing to eat. And there was nothing to drink. Outside, the wind howled like a coyote.

"Keep moving!" Mr. Miller ordered. The kids stamped their feet as they had on the playground earlier. They marched around. But they weren't getting ready to play fox and geese now. They jumped up and down. But they weren't trying not to be caught.

Instead, the children were playing a deadly game. If the little kids stopped, the bigger ones pulled them up, shook them, and slapped them. Everyone had to keep playing. Anyone who quit might be "out" forever.

Someone's waving arms broke a front window of the bus. More cold air and snow rushed in.

Sometimes the children had to rest. Rosemary held Maxine on her lap. Alice snuggled Laura and put her own coat around her little sister. Eunice wrapped her arms around Leland.

Poor Louise! Her sweater wasn't very warm over her cotton dress. And she didn't feel like moving around. She just sat quietly near the back of the bus where the snow was blowing in.

"Let's look around outside," Charles told Bryan. The two boys struggled into the blinding snow. In some places, the wind had swept the ground bare. In others, snow was drifting high. The boys couldn't see where land ended and sky began. It was as if they were watching a movie and the film had broken. All they saw was the blank white screen.

"Let's go back!" Charles called above the wind's roar. "Snow and dirt are hitting me in the face." The boys returned to the bus. They'd seen nothing. They were still lost. And they were even colder.

Now the kids were getting tired. They didn't feel like playing the horrible, grim game any longer. It was nearly bedtime. But Mr. Miller kept them moving. He pulled them up when they fell. He shook them. He rubbed their arms and legs.

Then darkness came—a blackness that made the children more scared. They could see nothing outside. They could see nothing inside. They were going to spend the dark night in a cold bus—lost in a blizzard.

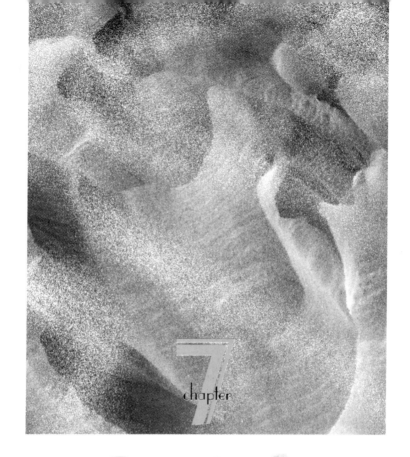

# Another Day—And Still Lost!

Friday, March 27, 1931

All night long, Mr. Miller tried to keep the children awake. He called them by name. He made them shout out one another's names.

For a short time, the children huddled close to keep warm. But then Mr. Miller and the older children would get everyone moving around. They were so tired. But they couldn't sleep.

Finally, daylight came. Everyone had been up all night. They'd had nothing to eat.

The wind was blowing at about 70 miles an hour. The snow was still swirling around the little bus. It was -20°F. That meant the windchill factor was lower than -85°F.

A foot or more of snow had invaded the bus. And the kids were exercising on top of it.

Mr. Miller was very, very tired. And he was cold. His clothes were wet from his trips outside to get fuel. Besides, Bryan was still wearing his jacket.

The bus driver looked at Louise. She was sitting as still as a statue. And little Mary Louise's eyes were glazed. She could hardly stand. If he didn't do something, they would all die.

"Bryan, I need my coat," he said. "I'm going for help."

Bryan returned his coat. Then Mr. Miller hugged and kissed Mary Louise. "Be brave. Daddy will be back," he said. "You big kids keep everyone moving! And we'll all be together for breakfast!"

The children watched Mr. Miller get off the bus. At once, he disappeared.

"He'll bring help soon," Rosemary said. She comforted Maxine and Bobbie.

## What To Do in a Blizzard

Have your home heating system checked every year. Listen to forecasts. Stock up on food and other supplies before the storm hits. Then stay at home during the storm. Do not go outside!

If you're traveling, make sure your car has a full tank of gasoline. Stop and find a safe place to stay inside.

If you're stuck in your car, stay there. Don't try to go for help.

1. If you leave the motor running, open a window slightly to avoid carbon monoxide poisoning.
2. It's often best to run the car's engine for a short period and then turn it off. This saves fuel.
3. Be sure the tailpipe is clear of snow.

However, if you must go outside, follow these safety rules.

1. Wear layers of clothing, boots, mittens (not gloves), and a warm hat that covers your ears.
2. Cover your face with a scarf or ski mask.
3. Follow something you can feel, such as a rope or fence.
4. Watch for fallen electrical lines.

Mr. Miller broke the most important rule for blizzard safety. Stay inside! Never go outside into the blowing snow!

"Keep moving!" Charles, Bryan, Clara, Rosemary, and Alice told the younger kids. But all they could do was stagger around the small bus on top of the snow. And that was only in the middle and front. The back was drifted full.

Then Rosemary noticed that her friend Louise had slid off the bench. She was sitting on the pile of snow. Her eyes were wide open. But she didn't move. Her face looked like stone.

"Wake up, Louise!" Rosemary shouted. The other kids joined her. They shook Louise. They slapped her face.

"Don't hurt my sister!" Blanche cried. Then she realized they were just trying to wake Louise up. But she wouldn't wake up.

She'll wake up after help comes, Rosemary thought.

Rosemary herself felt so tired! How much she wanted to sleep—just like Louise.

But still the children stumbled around. Then Kenneth fell at their feet.

"Don't go to sleep! Wake up!" they yelled at him. They tried to pull him up. They rubbed his arms and legs.

Kenneth told the others that his daddy was coming to get him. Then he slumped back down. The children put him in back with Louise.

Later they'll both wake up when it is warm, Rosemary thought.

Eunice's feet were swollen. She took off her shoes and put her overshoes back on. Now her feet were even more cold. And her hands were freezing as she held Leland close.

Max's rubber boots had filled with snow. His feet were freezing too. Alice's boots and mittens were so wet that they were freezing to her skin.

I'd be warmer without them, she thought. So she took them off.

To rest, the children huddled together for a while.

"Bobbie's going to sleep!" someone yelled. Bobbie was on a bench. His eyes were closed.

Rosemary hurried to her little brother! She joined the others rubbing Bobbie and pushing him around. But he wouldn't move.

"I'm warm now. Leave me alone," Bobbie said sleepily. The kids couldn't get him to move.

Since Mr. Miller had left, no one knew the time. Where was he? Why hadn't he brought help? It seemed as if they had been on the bus forever.

Some of the kids were barely awake. Maxine kept thinking she heard cars whizzing by. "Help! We're here!" she cried. But no one heard her voice.

About two o'clock in the afternoon, Alice and Rosemary thought they saw something outside. Someone was coming. They left the bus and staggered through a snowdrift. But they found nothing.

When the girls turned back, a sheet of snow slapped against them. Rosemary's feet felt like frozen sticks. Her icy dress cut against her knees like a knife. She pulled her long sweater sleeves over her hands.

Alice kept falling down. Each time, she could barely get up again. She was so tired—and so cold.

Back on the bus, Rosemary looked at Alice's hands. Her fingernails were black. Alice's hands were frozen.

# Frostbite and Hypothermia

The lost children suffered from **frostbite** and **hypothermia**. Frostbite happens when the skin freezes. The tissues become damaged. Usually the hand or foot tingles or becomes numb. If frostbite is not treated, tissues may die. The arms and legs may have to be **amputated**.

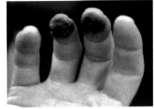

The children were also experiencing hypothermia. It occurs when body temperature falls below 95°F. People with hypothermia shiver. Their pulse rate becomes low. They move slowly. They're clumsy. They can't think straight. They may see and hear things that aren't really there. Finally, they may fall down or become so sleepy they just lie down. Eventually they die if help doesn't come.

"Let's lie down," someone suggested. Several of the children had removed their jackets and hats. They were feeling warm.

The older children decided to pile on top of the little ones. They'd keep one another warm. Maybe they'd even get some sleep.

But just then, Alice heard horses snorting. Charles heard the rattling of chains.

# Where Is Help?

When the blizzard began on Thursday, the children's parents didn't worry. Everyone knew how dangerous a prairie blizzard was. They were sure the teachers would keep the children at school.

For a while, Mary Louise Miller's mother waited for Mr. Miller. But when he didn't come, she decided that he, too, had stayed at school. Besides, there was nothing she could do. No one could go out in such a blizzard. She couldn't even get to the barn to milk the cows.

The wind howled like a hungry wolf. Snow flooded the air.

By Friday morning, Kenneth Johnson's parents decided the children would be hungry. Mrs. Johnson fixed food for everyone. Then Mr. Johnson took off for the school by horseback. The storm was still bad. In places, snow had drifted 10 to 12 feet high. But the horse snaked around the drifts.

At about the same time, Mr. Stonebraker hitched his horses to his wagon. He loaded Mrs. Stonebraker's handmade quilts and set out for the school. But when the men reached Pleasant Hill School, they discovered that the children weren't there.

But the children hadn't arrived home either. Where were they? They must be at someone's house. Or, too scary to believe, they might still be on the bus since yesterday morning. That was a long time in the freezing cold.

Mr. Stonebraker headed for the Untiedt home. On the way, he met Mr. Untiedt on horseback. He was looking for the children too. Mr. Untiedt tied his horse to the wagon and climbed in by Blanche and Louise's dad.

Inside the schoolhouse, after the blizzard

The men didn't have much time. Another night was coming.

Toward sundown, the wind let up. The snow quit blowing so hard.

Suddenly, the men saw something metal shining in a big pile of snow. Quickly, they rode up to the bus. It was stuck in a ditch beside the main road between Towner and Holly.

Snow was drifted against the door. Everything was very quiet. The men's worst fears seemed real. Everyone must be dead.

Mr. Stonebraker fixed his horses so they'd stay put. Meanwhile, Mr. Untiedt pushed through the drift. He tugged the door open. What a nightmare he saw! The back of the bus was filled with snow—three to four feet deep. Louise, Kenneth, and Bobbie were almost buried. It was too late for them.

The rest of the scene was almost as bad. In the front lay Arlo Untiedt. Next to him was Mary Louise Miller.

"Arlo! Arlo!" Mr. Untiedt called, lifting the little boy into his arms. But Arlo didn't move. Mary Louise remained still too.

In the middle, on top of a foot or more of snow, the other children were just beginning to pile on top of one another.

They'd forgotten Mr. Miller's orders. Or they'd been too tired to go on. Everyone was almost asleep.

Just then Mr. Stonebraker arrived. "Louise is dead," Mr. Untiedt told him.

"Oh, no! Oh, no!" he cried. "What about Blanche?"

Blanche was sitting near the door. Her garter belt had caught on the seat so she couldn't get up. She was almost asleep.

This newspaper photograph looks toward the rear of the bus, showing the aisle at center and the board bench and windows on the right. On the left, on a tipped-over bench, is the milk can lid in which the stranded passengers attempted to build a fire.

Charles and Maxine walked off the bus and climbed into the wagon. Quickly, the fathers carried the other children. Their arms and legs were stiff as icicles.

The men placed the children gently into the wagon and covered them with the quilts. Then they drove the horses to the nearest house.

Fern and Andy Reinert lived a half mile away. Fern was Eunice and Leland Frost's older sister. The Reinerts had a little boy too young to go to school. And Mrs. Reinert was expecting a baby.

1999 photo of Reinerts' house.

Charles and Maxine walked into the Reinerts' house. But the men carried most of the other youngsters. Their feet were swollen to twice their usual size. Their hands were frozen. And their skin was purplish red.

It was suppertime. Mrs. Reinert was frying potatoes on her coal range. The children had not eaten in over 33 hours.

The potatoes weren't cooked yet. But they smelled so good. The kids who could stand gathered around the stove.

Eagerly, Rosemary reached into the skillet and popped a mostly raw potato into her mouth. Charles had never tasted anything as good as those potatoes. Then he and his friends gobbled down a box of crackers. The men prepared soup and hot drinks for those who could swallow.

Fern Reinert tried to take off her little brother's overshoes.

"Don't pull them off!" Mr. Untiedt warned. He was afraid that removing the boots would tear at Leland's swollen feet.

At once, Mr. Stonebraker started helping Blanche thaw out. He moved her arms and legs, rubbing her with his hands. Gradually feeling returned to her back, right behind her heart.

The men and children had tracked lots of snow into the house. A good hot fire was burning in the stove, fueled by cow chips. But still the little house was damp and cold.

The men were worried about Mrs. Reinert and her little boy. Someone took them down the road to her parents' house. Only the men stayed to help the children thaw out.

Those fathers were strong ranchers. They'd seen livestock born. They'd seen livestock die. They'd killed animals for food. But to see their own children in such pain and danger was almost more than they could bear. Grown men were choked up. Some were openly crying.

When Mr. Johnson arrived, he learned that Kenneth was dead. At first, he couldn't stop the tears. But then he spent all night helping care for the other children.

The men removed the children's wet clothing and wrapped them in quilts. They put the children's frozen feet, legs, and hands in buckets of snow. They rubbed their limbs with salt. And they gave a spoonful of whiskey to some of them.

Four of the survivors are shown at the Reinert farm. From left to right: Laura Huffaker, Evelyn Untiedt, Ome Untiedt, and Max Huffaker

45

Then the men made the children sit up on the floor of the little house. They still didn't dare let the children sleep!

## Treatment of Frostbite and Hypothermia

Treatment of frostbitten or frozen limbs has changed since 1931. It is believed today that frozen arms or legs should not be rubbed. It's more likely that the skin tissue will die. Also snow and cold water make the body lose more heat.

Today, antibiotics and tetanus shots help to prevent infection. Here are suggestions to treat frostbite and hypothermia.

1. Carefully carry the person to a warm location. Sudden movement can cause death.
2. Remove all wet clothing and close-fitting items, like boots or gloves.
3. Put warm blankets around the person.
4. If the victim is awake, provide warm drinks, but no alcohol.
5. Although it's very painful, thaw the limbs as quickly as possible by putting them in warm water or a warm bath. Put warm towels on the person's neck and chest. Snuggle close to warm the person with your own body heat. However, keep the person away from a campfire or hot stove. Do not use a heating pad or hot water bottle. Skin might burn since the person has little feeling.
6. Get the person to a doctor or hospital as soon as possible.

If the victim has stopped breathing, today's treatment would include **cardiopulmonary resuscitation**.

How the children's arms and feet tingled and hurt as they thawed out! Rosemary felt as if little pins were sticking her. Blanche thought they felt like needles. The pain was awful. Most of the children were whining or moaning.

Sadly, it was too late for Mary Louise Miller and Arlo Untiedt. Even though the fathers tried to warm them, they wouldn't wake up. Like their three schoolmates, they had frozen to death.

While the children were recovering at the Reinert house, 50 to 60 men searched for Mr. Miller. Saturday evening, they found his frozen body.

Mr. Miller was lying face-up in the snow, his arms reaching out. He had walked more than 3½ miles from the bus.

When the men removed Mr. Miller's gloves, his hands were raw with cuts. He'd held on to a barbed wire fence while trying to find a farmhouse to get help.

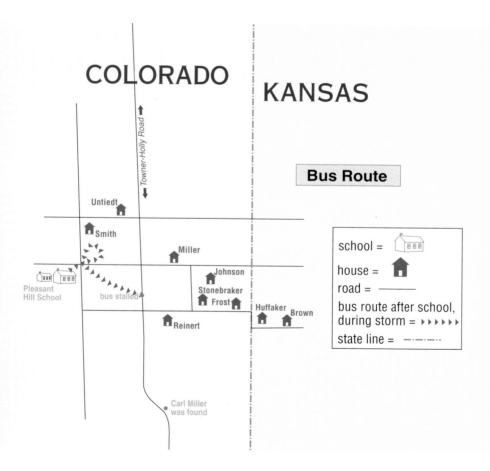

Meanwhile, the surviving kids needed a doctor. Someone rode horseback to the Stonebrakers' house. From there, he phoned the Huddleston **Mercantile** Store in Towner. But that store had no long distance lines.

Remains of Huddleston Mercantile Store. Photo taken in 1999

Howard Huddleston bundled up and walked to the home of W. P. Mayne. He owned the Mayne Mercantile Company. A long distance line was connected there.

## Rural Telephone Lines

In 1931, telephone messages were carried to ranches along the barbed wire fences. Fence posts about five feet high supported three rows of barbed wire. The messages ran along the middle row. Wherever the barbed wire was **spliced**, telephone wires connected the two parts so the message would get through.

Mr. Mayne placed a call to the Missouri Pacific Railroad office in Horace, Kansas. Would they send an engine and caboose to Towner to bring a doctor? The answer was "No." The drifts were too high for the train to get through.

Calls for help went to Holly, Colorado, and to Tribune, Kansas, north of where the Browns and Huffakers lived.

Someone even called the editor of the *Denver Post*. Would he send a plane with help for the badly injured children? But it was dark, and snow was still blowing. Even with burning buckets of kerosene to light the field, a plane could not land safely.

Sometime between 9 and 11 p.m. on Friday, eight men arrived from Holly. They had chained their automobiles together and plowed through the drifts. Among them was a doctor.

Meanwhile, 4 cars carrying 24 men left Tribune, Kansas. Some California tourists stuck in town joined the group. Another doctor was with them.

More men joined them in Towner. The men carried shovels to dig through the high drifts. Then, bumper to bumper, they pushed one another along.

The second group arrived at the Reinert house at about 11 p.m. The small house was so crowded that some of the men had to warm up in the henhouse.

However, the doctors needed medical supplies. Unless the children got more help, some might lose their frozen arms and legs. Or they might get **pneumonia**. Those most injured needed to go to the nearest hospital. It was about 50 miles away in Lamar, Colorado. There were no interstate highways. And the gravel and dirt roads were blocked by snowdrifts.

On Saturday, March 28, a small plane from Lamar landed in a field north of the Reinert house. Only three months before, pilot Jack Hart had flown to Tribune to play Santa Claus. This time he brought two nurses to care for the children. He then flew Alice and Blanche to the hospital. Alice had lain on top of two younger children. Her back and feet were frozen. Blanche was small and fragile. Her arms were frozen solid to above her elbows. Her legs were frozen up to her knees. The doctors expected both girls to lose their hands and feet.

Plane rescuing children

The editor of the *Denver Post* sent a second plane. Charles, Rosemary, and Bryan flew in that little plane. Charles enjoyed flying. He didn't know that many more "first" experiences were yet to come!

By Saturday evening, the roads were cleared. Laura and Max Huffaker went home. Their mom had just made doughnuts. Did they ever taste good!

Clara, Eunice, and Leland went to the home of the **mortician** in Holly. There, a doctor checked them.

"They'd all better go to the hospital," he said. "They still might get pneumonia." So the remaining children were driven to the hospital.

Remaining children being loaded into a vehicle that will take
them to the hospital

Blanche was in really bad shape. On Sunday morning, her
parents received a phone call. Blanche was not going to make
it, they were told. Quickly her mother went to the hospital.
Other mothers went to be with their kids too.

Survivior Bryan Untiedt with his
mother and mail addressed to
the surviors

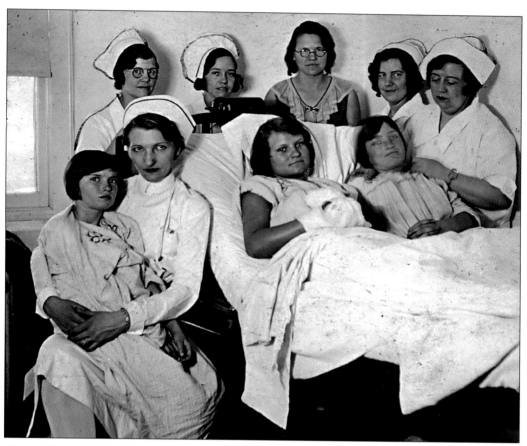

From left to right: Blanche Stonebraker, Alice Huffaker, and Rosemary Brown at the Lamar Hospital

The children spent two weeks at the Charles Maxwell Hospital in Lamar, Colorado. Being in the hospital was scary. Nobody knew if they would recover.

When nurses cut huge blisters off Alice's hands and legs, she couldn't feel anything. But as their frozen limbs thawed out completely, the children were in terrible pain. Luckily everyone, including Blanche, got better.

Three survivors wearing Easter dresses given to them in the hospital.
Front: Clara Smith and Rosemary Brown. Back: Alice Huffaker

Everyone was good to the kids and their parents. Mr. Charles Maxwell, mayor of Lamar, turned a floor of the hospital over to them. He didn't charge anything for their food, medicine, or care. Storekeepers gave the kids pajamas and other supplies. For Easter, they received new clothes. Store-bought clothes were very different from those their mothers had made!

Radios all over America broadcast the story of the children's horrible experience. Newspapers and **newsreels** told about them too. Reporters questioned the kids. Photographers took their pictures.

The United States was facing hard times in 1931. Many men had lost their jobs. Families didn't have much money. Life was difficult.

Yet people wanted to be happy. They were looking for heroes. So they turned the unlucky children who had survived the so-called Towner Bus Tragedy into heroes. Letters came from all over the world.

The name *Towner Bus Tragedy* is misleading since the bus served the Pleasant Hill School, not a school in the community of Towner.

The newspapers made a special hero of Bryan. They said that he had saved the other children. Some reported that he had given his clothes away to keep others warm. His classmates listened with surprise. Bryan had not done anything different from the others. But maybe it was easier for people to choose one hero rather than a busload of unlucky children who were at the wrong place at the wrong time!

Anyway, the kids didn't want to be heroes. What they had gone through had been terrifying. It was like an awful dream. They would never have chosen to be so cold—not even to become heroes.

# Mourning the Dead

The six headstones await placement at the Holly Cemetery. Bus driver Carl Miller was buried next to his daughter. Louise Stonebraker was buried on her fourteenth birthday.

At first, the survivors didn't understand what had happened to the other children—those who weren't at the hospital.

"Did Bobbie wake up?" Rosemary asked her mother one day.

Rosemary remembered how Bobbie had played house with Maxine. He had even carried her out of the broken glass when she had cut her foot. Rosemary and Maxine couldn't believe he was gone.

When Maxine got a nickel, she put it aside. She wanted to give it to Bobbie. She saved other treasures for him. When his casket was opened, she expected he'd come back to life.

Blanche Stonebraker didn't know that her sister, Louise, had died, either. "I thought she was asleep," Blanche said.

Tears of pain changed to tears of loss. But the children received no counseling. Rosemary's parents couldn't bear to talk about what had happened. Bobbie was gone—that was it. Instead, the pain and hurt were buried deep.

Wednesday, March 31, was a warm, sunny day. The birds were singing in Holly, Colorado. It was so different from just five days earlier.

But no one was enjoying the weather. The whole community was in shock. People were crying. It seemed as if life would never be okay again.

Holly schools and businesses closed. The senior play was postponed. Four ministers led a funeral service for Mr. Miller and the five children. Youngsters from the Holly school were **pallbearers** and flower girls. Overhead, National Guard airplanes dropped flowers. The bodies were buried together on a hillside in the Holly cemetery. Louise Stonebraker would have been 14 years old that day.

However, the survivors could not attend their classmates' funeral. They were still in the hospital.

But on October 7, 1931, the children went to a service **dedicating** a large new monument at the cemetery. On the monument were the names of their lost friends and siblings. Each who had died also had his or her own headstone.

Survivors surrounding the monument in the Holly Cemetery. They are:
1. Carl Huffaker, 2. Charles Huffaker, 3. Clara Smith, 4. Ome Untiedt,
5. Laura Huffaker, 6. Lena Huffaker, 7. Maxine Brown, 8. Max Huffaker,
9. Leland Frost, 10. Evelyn Untiedt, 11. Eunice Frost, 12. Rosemary Brown,
13. Alice Huffaker, 14. Bryan Untiedt. Missing from the photograph is
Blanche Stonebraker, who was still recovering.

Seven years later, a church was built where the bus had been stuck. The Towner Memorial Church opened at a ceremony on March 26, 1938. Each March, a special service was held to remember the awful event. Some of the survivors usually came. Beside the road, Carl Miller's brother placed a small block of cement that said, "Where the Bus Stalled in the Blizzard on, March 26 & 27, 1931."

Eventually the church moved to Towner. In 1962, the Towner Lions Club put up a marble monument where the bus tragedy had happened. Charles, Rosemary, and their friends Bryan and Ome Untiedt, Clara Smith Spear, and Blanche Stonebraker Widger attended the October service.

# chapter 10

# The Surviving "Heroes"

The survivors didn't return to Pleasant Hill School that year. Instead, the editor of the *Denver Post* invited them to Denver. Just three weeks after their terrifying experience, they rode to Denver in a special **Pullman** car. None of them had even been on a train before. Their parents came along as well as a doctor.

In Denver, Mayor Stapleton greeted the kids. Then they walked to fancy cars with uniformed drivers.

Many of the kids wore bedroom slippers on their swollen feet. They were limping. Rosemary walked with crutches. Someone carried Blanche. It all seemed very strange.

"The streets were lined with people just to see us. We were from the country. It was uncomfortable," Rosemary said later.

The cars took the kids and their parents to the fancy Brown Palace Hotel. The hotel's manager said in a newspaper interview, "We have reserved the best rooms in the hotel for them . . ." The hotel also planned a special dinner for the children.

Other restaurants gave the youngsters feasts too. Denver stores had them pick out new clothes. Then they had their pictures taken. That was very special. The families didn't have cameras at home.

One day, everyone went to an amusement park. The roller coaster made Alice feel sick. Then she was upside-down on another ride. With her hands bandaged, she couldn't hold on. She thought she would die. Then something good happened. She won a camera.

Charles had never been so far away from home. "They took us to the zoo," he remembered. "And to plays. And they had a special breakfast for us. They even got me my first date."

The children met the governor of Colorado and visited the state capitol.

The *Denver Post* gave each child a medal for heroism. It had the child's name and the date of the tragedy printed on the front.

"The *Denver Post* was really nice to us," Rosemary recalled. "I remember especially one breakfast. Each thing on the menu was named for one of us. I don't remember what I was. But it had my name beside it.

"After we had been to the zoo or somewhere else, they made us come back to the Brown Palace and drink **pasteurized** milk. We were all used to raw milk. We didn't like it."

Even along the train route home, people cheered the survivors. A large crowd met them when they returned to Holly.

The children also spent four days in Pueblo, Colorado. There they saw a ball game and visited a meat packinghouse. They were again honored at dinners and saw the newsreel of their hospital stay. Many people gave them gifts.

Even after all the honors they received, the kids didn't feel like heroes. To them, Mr. Miller was the real hero. He had kept them moving. He had given his life trying to save them. And their fathers were heroes too. They had rescued the children and kept them alive.

# 11

# Other Stories of the Storm

What had happened to the Pleasant Hill children coming from the west? The car carrying them got stuck in the snow near a farmhouse one quarter mile west of the school. The children and driver stayed safe in that house until the storm ended.

For a while, newspapers reported that a busload of children from a nearby town was also missing. On Saturday, March 28, they were found safe. They had also stayed at a farmhouse during the storm. Other children stayed at their schools during the storm.

On March 26, Edna Coons walked 1½ miles to the Kansas school where she taught. The blizzard came very suddenly.

Garry Waldren was driving his three children to the school. His car got stuck a half mile from there. He and the children held on to one another and walked safely to the school. They all shared Miss Coons's lunch and sat around the coal fire. They drank melted snow. Fortunately, the coal house was attached to the school. They were able to get fuel for the fire.

At another school, two of the students tied themselves together to go to the coal shed. After the coal supply was gone, the teacher burned the desks and seats.

North of Tribune, Kansas, a teacher kept her pupils for 29 hours. They had no food. After they were rescued, the roof fell in from the weight of the snow. Many people left their cars during the awful blizzard of March 1931. Today, we're afraid to let strangers into our homes. But people on the prairie survived because of the **hospitality** of people they didn't know.

A businessman and his friend walked four miles, following a barbed wire fence. Both men had frozen ears and legs.

But a family welcomed the men into their farmhouse. Sadly, the families of the men worried. Without telephones, the men couldn't call and report that they were safe.

In nearby Cheyenne Wells, Colorado, this author's father couldn't see his way home from work. He held on to buildings and fences.

Cheyenne Wells, Colorado, after the blizzard

One woman tied a rope around her son's waist and sent him to the barn to get a chicken. Then she pulled him in by the rope.

Another woman, living alone in the country, went to her barn and couldn't find her way back. She froze to death just a few feet from her kitchen door.

Lots of animals died in the Blizzard of 1931. "We saw frozen rabbits standing by fence posts," Miss Coons reported. Ranchers lost hundreds of cattle. Their noses were covered with ice and snow. So they smothered standing together in the fields.

Later the animals' bodies were piled and burned to prevent disease. Some ranchers had to give up farming because they lost so much in this storm.

# chapter 12

## NEVER Again!

Until the 1999 shootings at Columbine High School in Lakewood, Colorado, the Towner Bus Tragedy was the worst thing that had ever happened in a Colorado school system.

Families and neighbors who lived through it decided that schools should have fuel, water, food, and blankets to keep the children comfortable during a storm. One teacher remembers that the one-room school where he taught always had blankets, canned soup, and crackers on hand.

In addition, school systems made rules about when to send buses for children. School was often canceled if a storm was coming.

Soon after the Blizzard of 1931, buses had two-way radios. At least one bus in the area carried quilts, a small kerosene stove, and a can of kerosene. Sometimes the kerosene spilled, and the smell made the children sick before they reached the school. But it was a small sacrifice considering what could happen.

Front, left to right: Ome Untiedt, Max Huffaker, Bryan Untiedt, and Rosemary Brown. Other unidentified survivors are in back.

chapter 13

# And Then What?

The Pleasant Hill children had been through a terrible experience. Their lives would never be the same again. But they went on.

## ROSEMARY BROWN CANNON

Rosemary couldn't wear shoes most of the summer. After she could walk again, she took the exam to enter high school in Holly. There she sang in choruses and musical shows. She met her husband, Jack, while she was singing in an **operetta**.

On March 26, 1938, when the Towner Memorial Church opened, she gave birth to their son. Later, she and Jack had two daughters.

Rosemary always enjoyed dancing and singing. And she kept Alice, Eunice, and Blanche as her lifelong friends. But Rosemary never told her children about her frightening experience. It was too painful.

"I've spent a lifetime trying not to remember. But I can't forget," she said. "It left me with a feeling of guilt that we didn't save everybody. I have no idea what we could have done. Even the adults couldn't do anything for the two who died after we left the bus."

Later, she agreed to write about the event for a history book.

## CHARLES HUFFAKER

While in Denver with his schoolmates, Charles and his family met a salesman from Chicago. Each summer, their new friend visited their Kansas farm. At Thanksgiving and Christmas, Charles's dad sent the man a turkey. In return, the man sent presents to all the Huffaker kids.

In 1933, Charles's friend took him to the Centennial World's Fair in Chicago. Later, he helped Charles find a job in New York. After Charles married, he had three children—two girls and a boy.

Charles always remembered what had happened on March 26, 1931.

"If it had been 30 minutes later, we'd probably all have been asleep," he remembered about the rescue. "Thirty-three hours with nothing to eat and nothing to drink. It's amazing any of us were alive. It's a miracle, you might say."

But Charles didn't dwell upon the tragedy. "I just had to put it behind me and go on," he said.

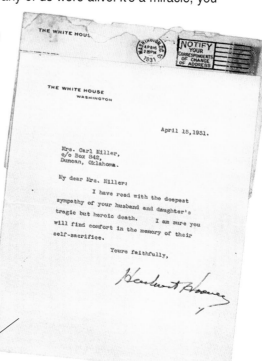

## MRS. MILLER

Mrs. Miller had lost both her husband and Mary Louise. Nothing could ever stop her pain and sadness. But the *Denver Post* raised $2,466.22 to help her. That was a lot of money in 1931! Each of the children's families received money for their pain and losses too.

Copy of the original letter sent to Mrs. Miller from President Herbert Hoover.

# Bryan Untiedt

President Herbert Hoover invited Bryan Untiedt to visit him in the White House. A clothing company gave Bryan a new suit. The president's son, Allan Hoover, gave Bryan a rifle. President and Mrs. Hoover gave him a set of harmonicas. And every year after that, Bryan received a Christmas card from President and Mrs. Hoover.

Bryan also gave a four-month series of lectures on the Pacific coast. There he met Tom Mix, a famous cowboy movie star. He also rode Arabian horses at the ranch of Mr. W. K. Kellogg, who made cereal.

Afterwards, Bryan attended high school for two years. Then he helped his father on the farm. He also took great pride in his black pony, Star. Later, Bryan became a builder in Denver.

Bryan Untiedt with President Hoover in Washington

## Blanche Stonebraker Widger

Blanche Stonebraker couldn't walk for three months after the accident. But she's always been able to discuss the bus tragedy.

"It was not caused by humans. It was just something that happened," she said.

## LELAND FROST

Leland Frost lived through the bus tragedy, but not through World War II. Leland graduated in 1941 from Towner High School. On June 4, 1943, he joined the United States Army. He served in General Patton's Third Army. After fighting in six major battles on the European Front, Leland was wounded in France on September 16, 1944. He died October 5, 1944, in a hospital in England.

In 1948, he was buried, with military escort and American Legion color guard, in the same cemetery as the friends he had lost in the bus tragedy. Later, his body was moved to another cemetery. Leland's parents received his **Purple Heart** after his death.

## ALICE HUFFAKER HUGGINS

After the bus tragedy, Alice Huffaker lost her fingernails and skin on her hands. For several years, her hands and feet would break out in a rash, crack, and bleed. They itched terribly. She lived in Holly to attend high school, working for room and board. Then she married and had three sons.

## LAURA HUFFAKER LOEHR

Laura Huffaker grew up and married too. Although she liked snow, she always panicked when a snowstorm caught her in a car.

Once she was in another blizzard. She just pulled a blanket over her head and waited to die.

## EUNICE FROST YOUKEY

Eunice Frost's legs swelled and broke out while the kids were in Denver. The doctor treated her. Later that summer she had a throat infection. She also had problems with her eyes—maybe from looking at the bright snow—and poor circulation in her feet and legs. For her whole life, she didn't like to go out in snowstorms!

# 14

chapter

## what's Left Today?

Mrs. Moser taught for only one year at Pleasant Hill School. During the 1940s, country schools like Pleasant Hill closed. Children living in rural areas were bussed to larger, **consolidated** schools.

The Pleasant Hill children went to school in Towner. The school buildings were sold and moved away.

What's there now where those children so long ago played their last carefree game of fox and geese? All that's left is the wind blowing through a field edged by sunflowers. On the ground lay some chimney bricks from the school.

Chimney bricks remaining from the school

The children's families eventually moved away too. Today, their houses are gone. But the home of Andy and Fern Reinert still remains to remind us of its sheltering arms on March 27, 1931. The Huddleston Mercantile Store, where the phone call for help was received, stands deserted in Towner.

In the Holly school yard stands a merry-go-round. It was a gift to the town from the meat packinghouse that the children visited in Pueblo and nine other businesses. A plaque reads "Lest we forget. This Karyor Merry-Go-Round dedicated to the 1931 heroes of Pleasant Hill School District #17, Kiowa County, Colorado."

The 1961 monument still marks the place where the bus stalled. Someone keeps artificial flowers there. On one side of the monument, the following words are written.

If you climb over the tumbleweed, sagebrush, and devil's claw, you can read the back too.

Mr. Miller's brother's stone sign remains there too.

| SURVIVORS |
| --- |
| ROSEMARY BROWN |
| MAXINE BROWN |
| EUNICE FROST |
| LELAND FROST |
| ALICE HUFFAKER |
| CHARLES HUFFAKER |
| LAURA HUFFAKER |
| CARL HUFFAKER |
| MAX HUFFAKER |
| LENA HUFFAKER |
| CLARA SMITH |
| BLANCHE STONEBRAKER |
| BRYAN UNTIEDT |
| EVELYN UNTIEDT |
| OME UNTIEDT |

Seventeen miles farther south, on a hillside in the Holly cemetery, stand the large monument and headstones for bus driver Carl Miller, his small daughter Mary Louise, and the four other children who froze to death on their way home from school. Now other members of their families have joined them to rest there for eternity.

Memories of the Blizzard of 1931 still haunt residents in eastern Colorado and western Kansas. Stories are passed down from parent to child.

Hillside of the Holly Cemetery

Rosemary once wrote, "Heroes they said we were, but I think it could be better put that we were simply victims of circumstances over which we had no control. Being children, as we were, we were not fully aware of the dangers we were facing, so we didn't panic as adults might have. Each of us did what we could, and by God's grace, some of us survived."

# GLOSSARY

| | |
|---|---|
| **adobe** | sun-dried clay brick |
| **almanac** | yearly publication that contains astronomical, statistical, meteorological, and general information. Many farmers and ranchers used the almanac as a planting and harvesting guide. |
| **amputate** | to cut off |
| **barometer** | weather instrument to measure air pressure |
| **barter** | to trade for goods or services without using money |
| **basin** | open circular container with sloping or curving sides used for holding water for washing |
| **blizzard** | snowstorm with winds at least 35 miles per hour and temperatures of 20°F or below |
| **borrow pit** | ditch or culvert by the side of the road |
| **bungalow** | small one-story house |
| **cardiopulmonary resuscitation** | method of bringing back breathing and heartbeat (CPR) |
| **coal oil** | liquid lamp fuel made from coal |
| **consolidated** | combined |
| **cow chip** | dried cow manure |
| **dedicate** | to establish something in someone's honor |
| **embroider** | to decorate with hand stitching |

| | |
|---|---|
| **frostbite** | damage done to skin and tissue when frozen |
| **garter belt** | elastic belt with fasteners to hold up stockings |
| **gunnysack** | bag made of coarse cloth |
| **hand-me-down** | clothing or other item put to use by one person after being used or discarded by another |
| **homestead** | to settle on land given by the government for farming |
| **horizon** | place where the sky and earth seem to meet |
| **hospitality** | friendliness toward visitors |
| **hypothermia** | below-normal body temperature |
| **lard** | fat from a pig used for cooking |
| **long handles** | two-piece long underwear |
| **lye** | harsh liquid made by washing water through wood ashes |
| **mercantile** | relating to trade |
| **meteorologist** | person who studies the atmosphere and forecasts weather |
| **mortician** | person who prepares bodies for burial |
| **newsreel** | short movies of current events shown along with feature films at movie theaters |
| **open range** | area without fences where livestock graze |
| **operetta** | romantic, comic opera with songs, dialogue, and dancing |

| | |
|---|---|
| outhouse | small building without running water that only contains a small bench with a cutout hole to be used as a toilet |
| oxford | low shoe that is laced or tied over the instep |
| pallbearer | person who helps carry a casket at a funeral |
| pasteurized | having been heated to kill organisms and germs |
| pneumonia | sickness in which the lungs are infected and fill with fluid |
| prairie | a large, flat area where grasses grow |
| prairie dog | rodent that lives underground in a colony |
| Pullman | railroad passenger car with seats that turn into beds |
| Purple Heart | military award and honor given to servicemen or their families who are injured or die in battle |
| reservoir | a container where liquid is stored |
| roan | dark-colored horse having a mixture of white hairs |
| running board | a footboard or step on the side of a vehicle |
| rural | having to do with the country, country people, or agriculture |
| satellite | artificial object that orbits around the earth, moon, or other celestial body |
| scorch | to burn |
| scuttle | shallow open basket or pail for carrying something |

| | |
|---|---|
| **separator** | machine to separate liquids with different weights, such as cream from milk |
| **slop** | to feed food waste to animals, especially pigs |
| **sod** | soil containing grass and its roots |
| **splice** | to join or unite by lapping two ends together |
| **starch** | to stiffen |
| **suffocate** | to kill by making one unable to breathe |
| **treadle** | foot-powereded pedal or lever that makes a machine work |
| **tumbleweed** | plant that dries up in fall, breaks off from its roots, and blows around |
| **washboard** | a board with ridges against which clothes are scrubbed |
| **weather vane** | metal figure, often in the shape of an animal, that rotates with the wind and shows its direction, often set on top of a building |
| **whitewash** | to paint with a mixture of lime, water, powdered chalk, and sticky glaze to make what is painted look clean and white |

# INDEX